SHOHE

*HOW JAPAN'S BABE RUTH BECAME THE MOST
ELECTRIC PLAYER IN MAJOR LEAGUE
BASEBALL*

By

JACKSON CARTER

Copyright © 2021

TABLE OF CONTENTS

Table of Contents

Legal Notes

Destined To Be Special

Trevor's Childhood Days

Trevor Cuts A Rug at Cartersville High

Gaining National Attention

Adjusting To A New Home

Stepping Into The Tigers Den

Living Up To Expectations

A Different Type Of Season

Getting Ready For The Biggest Night Of His Life

Trevor Tells Us Black Lives Matter

More From Jackson Carter Biographies

Other Works By Jackson Carter Biographies

LEGAL NOTES

Mac Jones is meant for entertainment and educational use only. All attempts have been made to present factual information in an unbiased context.

© 2021 Broad Base Publishing

All rights reserved. No portion of this book may be reproduced in any form without permission from the publisher, except as permitted by U.S. copyright law. For permissions contact:

BroadBasePublishing@Gmail.com

OHTANI IN A NUTSHELL

Shohei Ohtani is a famous Japanese baseball player who was born on July 5, 1994. He is currently 27 years old. He was born in Oshu, Iwate Prefecture, Japan. He is 6'4". He pitches with his right hand and bats left-handed.

He is colloquially known as Japan's Babe Ruth. He is just as good at hitting as he is at pitching. He started playing baseball because of his dad and quickly, the speed of his fastball started drawing attention both domestically and internationally.

First, he wanted to go to the United States directly after finishing school and skip the Japanese draft. However, the Hokkaido Nippon-Ham Fighters of Nippon Professional Baseball's Pacific League managed to get him to stay. He was their first pick in the draft of 2012. He played five seasons with the Fighters. He would bring them to the Pacific League Championship and Japan Series in 2016.

He has won multiple awards and holds the record for the fastest pitch by a Japanese pitcher in all of the history of BPH at 102.5mph.

In December 2017, he transferred to the United States on a contract with the Los Angeles Angels. Playing for them, he would go on to break numerous MLB records.

EARLY LIFE

Ohtani's dad, Toru, played baseball in Japan's corporate league. His mother, Kayoko, was a badminton player in the same corporate league.

They met at work because they worked in the same office. They have two children besides Ohtani, and they are Ryuta and Yuka. Ryuta is Ohtani's older brother. As a kid, he was a bit more withdrawn than Ohtani. He was scared of things that Ohtani wasn't scared of. But he always helped Ohtani practice baseball and they would race when they were young. All three siblings had a great relationship when they were younger and still do to this day.

He was born in a farm town called Oshu in the state of Iwate, where there are little to no urban centers but rice fields. It is roughly three hours north of Tokyo.

Oshu has a population of roughly 115,000 people and is about 400 square miles.

It is known for its delicious beef, festivals, temples, and Fujiwara no Sato. Fujiwara no Sato is a theme park based on the 1000s.

It has very fertile land for farming. It has rivers and mountains. It has hot summers and cold winters.

Many people from Oshu dream of moving to Tokyo when they grow up, and work hard to escape the country in exchange for city life. They don't want to be farmers like their parents and would prefer to live in a big city with more opportunities.

However, Ohtani never had that dream. He loved growing up where he did and found joy in the open fields. Although his parents weren't farmers and worked in a corporate office, he didn't see any problem with living in Oshu. But his sights were set on America once he started to get really good at baseball.

Ohtani's father says he was always very engaged and curious about his interests. He would try out new things, to the point that you had to really keep your eye on him because sometimes he would push his limits to a dangerous level.

He was adventurous from a very young age. His older brother was too scared to play on the playground, but Ohtani would happily play on it. He wasn't scared of falling or breaking bones. He was incredibly coordinated with both fine and gross motor skills. He ran around freely and found a way to have fun no matter what he was doing.

He also saw small details. At one time he got upset because his notebook had a tiny wrinkle and insisted that someone must have touched it. His father tried to teach him at that moment not to sweat the small stuff.

Ohtani was both very social and very withdrawn. He was especially adventurous when it came to sports and competitions. He loved playing tag with his friends and was always the fastest. He bored quickly because no one was as good as him.

He was also in his own world, thinking hard about life and caring deeply about things. He got upset easily. This is because he cared so much and paid attention to the little things. He didn't understand why people weren't kind. He was taught incredible manners, so it shocked him when people were rude. It took him time to learn to control his temper as a child. But with his parents' guidance, he learned to be more emotionally disciplined.

In all, Ohtani had an incredible childhood. He was able to have a lot of fun playing games and sports with his siblings and parents. He learned valuable life lessons in a wonderful household. His family was middle class and he never lacked food or shelter. His early childhood helped shape the trajectory of the rest of his life: being kind yet hardworking.

As a toddler, Ohtani's favorite thing was to play on the playground swingset. He loved being pushed to his limits and seeing how high he could swing. It was always a competition for him—he always insisted that his mom or dad swing next to him so that he could see who could swing higher. Once he was old enough, he stopped asking to be pushed and enjoyed doing it all by himself.

He loved the swings so much that his parents got a playground for their backyard. He would climb up the slide and then slide down it. He was like a real monkey on the monkey bars. He would never slowly end the swing; he would always jump off of it at its highest point. He would slide down the railing.

He and his siblings loved playing pretend on the playground. Their favorite game was playing lasers. This was like imaginary laser tag. They would run around the playground hiding from each other and threw balls at each other to get each other out. Ohtani was very good at this game because he was so fast and had such good aim. His siblings had fun but always lost.

THE START OF A LEGENDARY CAREER

Ohtani began to play baseball during year two of elementary school. He started to become fascinated with baseball after he went to see a baseball game in person. Seeing the home runs go out of the stadium lit a fire inside of him. He loved the energy of the crowd and imagined being in the field playing with people cheering him on. He was especially enamored with pitching and hitting. He wondered how people threw the ball so fast or hit it so far. He decided he wanted to be as good as them.

He loved gym class. No matter what sport, he excelled, especially sports that involve throwing things. He was always the fastest student. He was the tallest in his grade for his entire life. He would go home and talk about gym class nonstop, recalling every detail of the game.

However, he was taught to be a good sport. Even though he always won, he never bragged or rubbed it in. He congratulated the losing team just as much as he did the winning team. He would smile but not celebrate too hard so as to avoid hurting feelings. He saw sports as something to have fun with as well as practice and become better at.

He also cared about his studies. His parents instilled in him discipline and a love of learning. He would come home every day and do his homework, even if it took him hours to complete. His parents helped him with his work.

Teachers already knew of him because of his older siblings, so he had a leg up. His family had a good legacy within the school. This is because of how well his parents raised him and his siblings. They were well behaved and good students as well as good classmates. They helped other students. They asked good questions. They always handed their assignments in on time. It was a pleasure to have them in class.

In middle school, he joined the Ichinoseki Little Senior baseball league. This was roughly 45 minutes away from his home. His dad happily made the drive for him and also became a coach for the team. He partially wanted to coach because he felt as though he let his other son down because he was working so much and wasn't able to train so much with him. He wanted to be better for Ohtani.

Toru was a thorough coach. He told his son to keep his form clean when he pitched and to make sure his fingers had a firm grip on the seam of the ball. When batting, he told him to hit with the center of the bat and helped him to develop his skills as both a right and left hitter.

He also told Ohtani not to get angry and throw his equipment if he didn't perform the way he had wanted to. He wanted to teach his son that objects had value, as well as that outburst made the rest of the team have lower morale. This temper was leftover from Ohtani's childhood. It stemmed from him wanting to do incredibly well at everything he did. He learned over time that it required hard work and dedication, as well as patience. He hated when he made mistakes, but learned that it is okay not to be perfect. Having a well-balanced attitude of drive as well as forgiveness shaped how Ohtani trained for the rest of his life.

In the car, on the way back from practice, even if there had been a point of conflict during training or if training didn't go as planned, Toru didn't lecture Ohtani. He worked night shifts and dinner time was important to him. They usually talked about baseball over dinner.

Ohtani's family was incredibly supportive of everything he did. They taught him to be caring, disciplined, and to always have fun. He had a quiet nature but that didn't stop him from his adventures.

From a very young age, his parents knew he was special. Having been a bit absent for his older brother's upbringing, they wanted to really get it right with Ohtani. They nourished his skills and tried to teach him through positive reinforcement rather than punishment.

Ohtani had a good relationship with his siblings. They had a healthy sibling rivalry and would always play together as well as study together. His older brother helped him with his schoolwork and played catch with him once he started to really focus on baseball.

While his dad decided to coach his baseball team and really be present in that area of Ohtani's life, his mom nurtured his personality lovingly. She taught him what was important in life. She took care of the family by doing grocery shopping, cooking, and cleaning. She instilled a sense of responsibility in Ohtani by having him help with chores.

TAKING IT TO THE NEXT LEVEL

By now, Ohtani was on a strict practice routine. On top of having practice five days a week for his league, he would also go to the batting cages on the weekends and his dad continued to help him with his pitching form. He also did strength training in the mornings.

Baseball focuses on short, intense movements rather than prolonged stamina like soccer. This is also why there are often so many injuries in baseball. Because of this, the focus of training for baseball is not to bulk up. It is to create power for when you hit or throw.

Training for baseball should focus on making acceleration better, as well as, instead of exercising the shoulders, working on supporting muscles.

One exercise Ohtani did was the backward twisted lunge. It helps protect the lower back and stretches the hip flexors. It increases mobility while throwing. He stepped back into a lunge, lifted his arm up, and twisted his torso, repeating the routine on both sides.

Another exercise he did was a drop lunge. It makes the hips more flexible. He turned his hips and reached back with his foot, with his left toes facing his right heel. He rotated his hips to face forward and lowered into a squat.

He also did leg cradles. It extends the glutes and hips, which are used for all movements in the sport. He lifted his foot off the ground and squatted. Then he pulled his knee into his chest.

Lastly, he did the medicine ball rotation throw. This helps improve acceleration in the hips, which is helpful for both batting and throwing. He stood facing a wall that was solid, roughly three feet from the wall. He held the ball at his waist and rotated his hips from the wall. Then he threw the ball by rotating his hips, then his trunk, then his arms, and lastly the ball.

The Summer Koshien is where Japanese legends are born. Ichiro Suzuki was put on the map in 1991 at the Koshien. Daisuke Matsuzaka pitched a no-hitter in '98. He threw 250 pitches in 17 innings. Yankee player, Masahiro Tanaka, threw 742 pitches over the course of 52 innings in six games at the tournament in 2006.

The Summer Koshien is officially called the National High School Baseball Championship of Japan. It is a yearly nationwide baseball event for high school teams that dates back to 1915. It happens during summer vacation when the players are free to train and play. It crescendos into a two-week-long final competition in August with almost 50 teams. Each team represents one of Japan's prefectures.

Although his team didn't win, Ohtani was burst into the headlines when, only a few days before he turned 18, he threw a fastball that was 99mph. This created a record for any Japanese pitcher who was in high school.

This fastball was no accident. He had been training ever since middle school to perfect his speed and form, especially with the help of his dad, special trainers, and his own strength training. Everything paid off on that fateful day. The stars aligned because throwing it at the Summer Koshien meant getting national coverage rather than just throwing it at a normal game, although he very well might have thrown that fast at a normal game and no one knew it. No matter what, throwing that fastball really started his professional career in the end.

How to Understand Baseball Stats and Terminology

At Bat (AB)

At Bat counts how many times a player bats. But being walked, doing a sacrificed play, and being hit by a pitch don't count. So AB is how many times you're at the plate when other things happen, like getting a hit.

Run Batted In (RBI)

An RBI is when someone scores because of your hit. For example, if there's someone on second base and your hit brings them home, you get an RBI.

Batting Stats

Batting stats consist of the batting average (BA or AVG), the on-base percentage (OBP), and slugging (SLG). These stats are usually all in a row with a slash in between them. So it goes BA/OBP/SLG.

The BA is when you have someone's total number of hits and divide them by their AB. There can be a BA for a game or for the season. But when seen between the slashes, it typically represents the season unless stated otherwise. An incredible BA is .300, which means you still miss seven out of ten opportunities to get a hit.

Your OBP is sometimes considered more important than the BA. This is because it includes walks and other things that a BA doesn't.

Slugging is more complicated. It is all the bases, including the extra-base hits, divided by the AB.

THE NEXT LEVEL

Now was the time to decide if Ohtani wanted to pursue baseball in college, move to a professional Japanese league, or try to move to America to play in the MLB. He was very studious and liked the idea of being able to study and play ball.

But his parents and friends pointed out that he would be spread thin traveling for college ball while also studying. He also wasn't sure what he would want to go to school for. After considering whether he wanted to play in Japan or America, he set his eyes on the MLB.

The Hokkaido Nippon-Ham Fighters drafted Ohtani even though they knew he most likely wouldn't play on their team. But he decided to sign with them and play in Japan before moving to America to play for the MLB.

Hokkaido gave Ohtani the opportunity to be both a position player and a pitcher. Meanwhile, the Los Angeles Dodgers were not going to let him do that. He wanted to be both a position player and a pitcher, and although the Los Angeles Dodgers were his first choice, he followed his desires and stayed in Japan.

He also considered the repercussions of playing in minor league baseball. It was a way to prepare for the major leagues, but it had a little immediate payoff, long hours, he would be away from home, and he wouldn't be playing the positions he wanted. It would also give him less time to prepare to move to America.

His jersey was the number 11.

Even though he said he was going to give up his opportunity to go professional in the country of Japan and go to the MLB instead, and he was rumored to have offers from many teams, they then drafted him as their number one in the NPB Draft of 2012.

Over a month, the team of Nippon-Ham had a well-thought-out plan to get Ohtani to play for them. They developed a long-term sales pitch that they named "The Path to Realizing Shohei Ohtani's Dream." It was about what he could do with the Fighters as well as what minor league play in America really looks like.

They made a video showcasing reality, like not having Japanese food, long bus rides, and being away from his family.

It also showed that he would become instantaneously famous if he stayed in Japan, and how his friends and family would be around. They said they would prepare him, helping him with his training to eventually move over to the MLB.

Nippon-Ham took a huge risk by choosing Ohtani as their first pick. That's why they committed so much energy to get him to realize his potential in Japan. They really stuck their necks out to get Ohtani to play for them. They were strategic and thorough, hitting on all the points they knew would be important to him.

Without the Fighters, who knows what would have happened in Ohtani's career.

A ROOKIE SEASON TO REMEMBER

In 2013, he debuted at 18 years old in the Fighter's first game of the season on March 29, 2013. He played in the right field.

He was chosen in the Pacific League for the 2013 All-Star Game. He pitched and ended his season with a 3 to 0 record in 11 starts. In his first year, he played the outfield and as a pitcher. He played 51 games in the right field.

He was only the second Nippon Pro Baseball rookie who played directly out of high school as a pitcher and in a position. He was out for most part of the season because he sprained his right ankle and fractured his right cheekbone.

He was the first pitcher besides Takao Kajimoto to bat 3rd through 5th and the very first rookie hurler to do that ever since Junzo Sekine in 1950. He played as the second person, after Osamu Takechi, in 1950, to start as the pitcher, bat between 3rd and 5th, and get a hit and Run Batter In.

He was voted into the All-Star Game even though his numbers weren't amazing.

This is because he is so talented and such a good sport. Even though his numbers didn't show it, everyone saw his talent and potential, especially after his record-breaking pitch in high school. It was obvious that he was just thrown off by playing in a new setting. He was beloved by both his fans and teammates, as well as his coaches. He is a great person to play next to and that earned him a spot on the All-Star team.

GETTING COMFORTABLE

During his second year, he both pitched and played in the outfield. He was great at throwing the ball and also very good at hitting it. His average was .274. He had 28 hits that were extra-base. He had a total home run count of 10. He had 31 Run Batter In's and a .842 percentage on the bases. He batted 212 times.

When he pitched, his record was 11-4. He had a 2.61 ERA and started 24 times. He struck out 179 times. The number of innings he pitched was 155. His strikeouts were third in the National Pacific Baseball League. The people batting while he pitched had an average of only .223.

In a game versus the Orix Buffaloes, he became the first Japanese player to get digits in the doubles in wins as well as home runs. He pitched a 1-0 game and became the first pitcher directly from high school to get a 1-0 shutout win during his first two years with the Fighters since Toshiaki Moriyasu did it in 1967. He was also the first pitcher who didn't go to college to get two shutout wins in his first two years in the National Pacific Baseball League after Yu Darvish.

In the 2014 All-Star Game in July, Ohtani threw a 101mph pitch in the 1st inning, which broke the 2010 record of 100mph. The shirt he wore when he made that pitch sold for $17,000. That made it the most expensive item at the All-Star 2014 Charity Auction. All the money went to three earthquake relief funds.

On October 5th, he pitched the fastest ball by a Japanese player during an official game and tied the record for National Pacific Baseball. It was during the first inning and was 101mph. It broke the batter's bat. He threw 15 pitches in the first inning, eight of which were in the 99mph range.

In his postseason, he was picked to be on the national team called Samurai Japan, and played in the All-Star series. It was a friendly five-game series that consisted of major league players.

In the first game, he pitched a relief inning and retired three batters consecutively. He started the fifth game. Even though they lost, he wasn't charged with an earned run. He made 12 outs in four innings and seven of them were strikeouts. He mostly pitched fastballs, including one that was 99mph. He threw a few curveballs and forkballs.

During the 2014 season, Ohtani focused on expanding the range of his pitches and mastering more than just the fastball. Even in high school, he had a wicked-fast fastball. But now that he was in a major league, just pitching fastballs wasn't going to work. He learned how to throw changeups, curveballs, cutters, knuckleballs, forkballs, and knuckle curves. Although he wasn't perfect at each pitch, it was important for him to begin to expand his palette to challenge his batters more and make him a more desirable player when the time came to be drafted for the MLB.

2015 was his third pro season and second full season. His batting wasn't as good and he got five home runs. But his pitching was some of the best in all of the NPB. He started in the 2014 All-Star Game and won in pitching in the Pacific League Best Nine awards.

He went 2 innings and fanned 2, letting in one run, which was on a double and a single. The PL lost 8-6, but he still got a no-decision. He finished the season 15-5. He had a 2.24 ERA. He also made 196 strikeouts and only let up 100 hits while pitching 160 innings.

He got third in Most Valuable Player voting behind Tanagita and Shogo Akiyama. But he placed first among all the pitchers. He was one of the three people who were considered for the 2015 Sawamura Award, which was given to the best pitcher every year.

He led in wins and winning percentage with a record of 15-5 and 22 starts. He had a 2.24 WEA. He played 5 full games and 3 shutouts. These were all the best of his career, just like his 196 strikeouts, 11 strikeouts every nine innings, and .909 WHIP.

He was the best for the Japanese team in the 2015 Premier 12. He threw 100mph and destroyed South Korea (who eventually won the championship) before their relief pitcher. He faced South Korea for the second time in the semifinals. He had 11 K, 0 BB, 1

HB, and 1 H in seven innings pitched. He had the most whiffs in one game for the first Premier 12.

His relief pitcher let in four runs in the 9th inning when Japan shockingly lost. He was the top of the event in ERA and strikeouts and had the lowest average for a starting pitcher. He was named the All-Star SP.

At this point in his career, he was starting to find his footing. Although he was still struggling in some areas, he was also excelling in others. He was also starting to win awards and break records for the first time since high school. He would go on to become very familiar with this pattern, always pushing himself for the next record or the next opportunity. During this season, he was growing as a player and his potential was starting to shine through.

2016: An MVP Season

In 2015, Ohtani played 104 games. He was at the plate 382 times and hit 22 home runs, along with 18 doubles, and 67 RBI. He batted .322 with an OBP of .416. He made 65 runs and stole 7 bases. He got the Best Nine award as a designated hitter.

He had another great season on the mound. He pitched 21 games. He had the lowest in his career in ERA with a score of 1.86. His record was 10-4. He struck out 174 batters in 140 innings. He had four full games and one shutout. He won the Best Nine as a pitcher as well and also the Pacific League MVP. He got almost double the number of votes as any of the other pitchers in the PL for the 2016 NPB All-Star Game.

He couldn't pitch during the series because he had a blister on his finger but shined as the designated hitter. In the first game, he lined out in the 8th inning. He started as a designated hitter and hit 5th in the second game. He started the PL comeback from a 3-0 score in the 5th inning. He singled in the 7th and scored on a hit by Kenta Imamiya to make it a 4-3 lead. They were behind 5-4 in the eight, but he brought someone in with the run that tied the game. He made three out of five runs in the tie game, which got him the game MVP. He hit 102.5mph, which was an NPB record.

He finished off the season with .332/.6/.588 and RR HR in 382 PA. He also recorded 10-4, 1.86 pitching, and 174 K in 140 innings pitched. He tied for 8th in the PL for wins and was third in the number of strikeouts.

He brought Nippon Ham to the 2016 Japan Series. They lost the first game to the Hiroshima Carp. He fanned a total of 11 in just 6 innings, but he let in three runs. Two were from a home run and one was a steal of home plate. He was down 2 games to 0. But he did a great job as the designated hitter in the third game. He got three hits, a run, and an RBI. In the bottom of the 10th, he won the game, and Nippon Ham would win the following three games and win their second Japan Series title. He hit .375/.412/.625. He hit four doubles and helped more offensively than as a pitcher in the Series.

He made the Best Nine as the best pitcher and the best designated hitter in the PL. He was the very first player to get the awards as both a pitcher and a hitter. He was the nearly-unanimous winner of the 2016 Pacific League MVP Award; he got 253 out of 254 votes. He had a total of 1,268 votes. His next runner-up had 298.

In his 2016 season, he was beginning to really show what he was made of. Continuing to win awards, his pitching and batting averages were incredible. A .322 batting average is way above the average and is considered excellent by everyone's standards. He won awards as both a hitter and a pitcher, starting to solidify what he would eventually be called—Japan's Babe Ruth. It is incredibly uncommon for pitchers to also be good at hitting. But for Ohtani, being good at one helped him also become good at the other because he understood the mind games that both pitchers and batters play.

2017 SEASON AND GETTING POSTED

In 2017, Ohtani played 65 games. He hit a .332 with eight home runs and 31 RBIs. He went 3-2, 3.20, and pitched 29 strikeouts.

In September, it was announced that he would be posted at the end of the 2017 season to play in the MLB in 2018. But before that could happen, he had surgery on his right ankle in October. His right ankle injury had first happened in the 2016 Japan Series and had ruined his chance of playing in the 2017 World Baseball Classic. It also restricted his ability to play during the regular season.

It was wondered if the NPB and MLB could create a posting agreement. They both agreed on November 21, 2017.

Since he was under the age of 25 years old, he was subject to international signing rules. This made his bonus to be capped at about $3 million, putting him on the rookie salary scale. The signing team additionally had to pay a $20 million fee to his current team. That meant that all 30 teams were monetarily able to get him.

It is thought that if he had waited until he was the age of 25 to get posted, he would have had a $200 million many-year-long contract, although no team had come forward with an offer that big.

He narrowed his eyes on many teams. He signed with the Angels with a roughly $2 million bonus.

Things were starting to really happen for Ohtani. His whole life had led up to this moment. He loved sports as a child and began to develop his skills, including his competitive side, his discipline, his ability to have fun, and his good sportsmanship. The training he began to receive in middle school both bonded him with his father and prepared him to undergo rigorous training later in life. His high school career ended with a bang with his record-breaking fastball. And then with The Fighters, he went on to break numerous records and win a slew of awards. It was time for all that hard work to pay off and for him to finally reach his goal of playing for the Angels.

Japanese Posting System

People who play in the Nippon Professional Baseball League, or NPB, who don't have nine years playing for the league that is required to have international free agency, can ask to be posted for the MLB.

There is something called a release fee. That is how much an NPB club gets if a player makes a deal with a Major League club. It depends on how much the contract is worth.

There is a 30-day window to make negotiations with someone once they are posted. This usually happens between November 1 and December 5.

If there is no contract developed in that window, the person who was posted goes back to their NPB club. They can't be posted again until the next offseason.

There are different release fees depending on the amount of the contract. The percentages vary.

MOVING TO THE MLB

At the age of 23, everyone in Japan was obsessed with the pitching and hitting star, Shohei Ohtani. It was now time to move to America and play in the MLB. He was well known in the MLB world for his incredible fastball and slider as well as his hitting skills, and how he brought his teams to victory so many times in Japan. He was also known for how he and his agent sent a questionnaire to all 30 MLB teams in an attempt to find the best fit for his individual skillset.

He was obsessed with baseball during his time with the Fighters and did nothing but get ready for the MLB. He lived in the Nippon-Ham housing to be closer to training gyms. He exercised daily and ate incredibly well. He didn't go out with his teammates and didn't date so that he could focus on baseball. He studied English a lot.

Now it was time to make the big move. Ohtani spent a lot of time with family and friends to get ready to say goodbye and move to America. When he wasn't playing baseball, he was watching baseball, and when he wasn't watching baseball, he was either with friends and family or studying English.

He was ready to make a splash in the MLB, although he may not have known just how big of a star he would go on to be. It's impossible to know if he had any idea what his life would turn into once he got to the major leagues. Although it took a few seasons for him to fully find his footing, just as he did with the Fighters, he would go on to become a legend, with more still to come.

The Los Angeles Angels are out of Los Angeles and its surrounding area. They are part of the American League West. They play home games at Angel Stadium, located in the town of Anaheim. This has been going on since 1966.

The team was first owned by Gene Autry in 1961. He was a cowboy singer who was immensely popular as both a singer and an actor, and was in many films through the 30s to the 50s.

They were named the Angels after the original Los Angeles Angels, which was a Minor League team between 1903 and 1957. He bought the rights to the name.

Throughout the team's history, their win-loss record is 4,735-4,752, which gives them a .499 average.

They have a mantra of "Win One for the Cowboy." This is because the team's first owner never saw them win a World Series even though he owned the team for 38 years. The first time they won the World Series was in 2002, four years after Autry's death.

Their stadium is lovingly called "The Big A." In center field, they have a display called the "California Spectacular." It is a group of fake rocks designed after the mountains of California. It has a waterfall that runs and releases fireworks before each game and each time the Angels get a home run or win a game at the stadium.

Their mascot is the Rally Monkey.

2018 SEASON: A ROOKIE AGAIN

Ohtani was part of a 25-man roster and was the designated hitter on Opening Day playing the Oakland Athletics. He got a single in his very first MLB at-bat.

On April 1, he pitched in the MLB for the first time. He struck out six batters during six innings and let up three runs, making it his first MLB win.

On April 3, he hit his first home run in the MLB. It was a 397-foot three-run home run against pitcher, Josh Tomlin. The very next day, he hit his second home run, which made him the first Angels player to hit a home run during both of his first two career games on home turf.

He tied the Angels record of 12 bases and five RBIs in the first three consecutive games of his career. Both of these records were set by Bobby Clark in 1979.

On April 6, he hit his third home run in only three days. That made him the first Angels rookie to ever do that.

During his second start as a pitcher on April 8, he played a perfect game for 6 innings before letting up a hit. He pitched seven innings with no scores and struck out 12 people.

On April 18, it was his third start pitching, but he had to stop after two innings because he had a blister on his middle finger on his right hand. On June 7, he left the game for the same blister again. The next day, he was put on the disabled list because of a UCL sprain in his right elbow. He got platelet-rich plasma and stem-cell injections as a treatment.

Platelet-rich plasma, or PRP, injects a concentrate of one's platelets to speed up healing. These injections are prepped by taking blood and processing it through a centrifuge. This concentrates all the platelets. Then they are injected right where you need them. Sometimes ultrasound is utilized to guide where they are injected.

He left the disabled list to hit on July 2 but was 0 for 4 playing the Seattle Mariners.

On August 3, he hit two home runs facing the Cleveland Indians, which made it the first game in his career where he hit multiple home runs. They were also his first two home runs away from their home stadium.

After not pitching for 11 weeks, his manager, Mike Scioscia, said that he would start on September 2 against the Houston Astros. He threw 49 pitches in 2 innings and let in two runs. But he became the first MLB player in almost 100 years to hit 15 home runs and pitch 50 innings in one season, which Babe Ruth did in 1919.

On September 7, he broke the Japanese rookie home run record with 19 home runs thus far in the season.

He ended his first MLB season with a .285 batting average and a .361 on-base percentage. He ended up with 22 home runs and stole 10 bases. He also had 61 RBIs. He started the game on the mound 10 times with a 4-2 record. He had a 3.31 ERA as well as a 1.16 WHIP. He made 63 strikeouts.

He had a slugging percentage of .564, which made him number seventh among all the MLB players who had at least 350 times at the plate that season. He was the second-fastest Angels rookie to reach 20 home runs. He and Babe Ruth are the only two MLB players who pitched 10 games and hit 20 home runs in the same season. He won the American League Rookie of the Month award both in April and September.

On September 3, 2018, ESPN stated that doctors wanted Ohtani to get a Tommy John surgery when an MRI revealed his UCL damage. On September 25, the Angels let the world know that he would be getting the surgery, which would keep him from pitching until 2020. Luckily, he had a successful surgery. On November 12, 2018, he was awarded the American League Rookie of the Year.

During just his first year, he was a huge deal, winning the American League Rookie of the Year, which is a huge honor. He got a single in his very first at-bat against an MLB pitcher. He tied a record with Babe

Ruth. A .285 batting average is admirable. He was having no trouble adjusting to the big leagues. It was clear that staying in Japan to play for the Fighters had paid off, as he was now ready to take on his career in America.

What Is Tommy John Surgery?

Tommy John Surgery is formally referred to as Ulnar Collateral Ligament Reconstruction or UCL reconstruction. It is implemented to completely repair a damaged UCL inside the elbow, which is found on the inner or inside elbow, and helps to secure and protect the joint inside the elbow.

It is especially popular among athletes, especially in sports where you have to throw the ball because that can overuse the UCL.

For UCL reconstruction, you have to harvest a tendon that comes from either your body or a kind donor and attach it to the elbow as a replacement UCL.

It might take over a year to get back to full strength and be as good of an athlete as you were before the procedure.

The surgery wasn't invented by a man named Tommy John. Rather, he was a pitcher in baseball who became the very first person to get the surgery and go back to playing his sport.

Tommy John surgery is incredibly common among pitchers. And while it can put a career on hold, it often doesn't end the career. It is especially common among pitchers who have high pitch counts. That is part of why pitchers try to keep their pitch counts low to avoid injury. But it is a safe procedure that is often mandatory for pitchers and will allow them to keep playing the game they love.

Recovery From Tommy John Surgery

Immediately after the surgery, the elbow is put into a brace at an angle somewhere between 60 and 90 degrees. PT is started on surrounding areas to avoid the muscle from deteriorating and losing strength.

After one or two weeks, you can move your elbow again. You might have a brace that is on a hinge that you can lock at an angle when you're not exercising. You might wear a sling on your arm if it's more comfortable. PT will focus on slowly getting a larger motion range inside the elbow at this point of recovery.

You might be able to completely straighten the elbow and stop wearing your brace by the end of your first month of recovery. With consistent PT, you can probably get back your normal motion range between two and four months post-surgery.

Athletes will typically take between six and nine months to get back into their sport after surgery.

While it is hard to wait so long to get back to your sport, it gives you time to reset your mind and create new goals for yourself. A lot of athletes have trouble adjusting from their rest period back into gameplay. But Ohtani took the opportunity to continue to study the sport, watch his favorite pitchers and batters, and set goals.

2019 Season: Bouncing Back

On May 7, 2019, Ohtani played his first game since his surgery as the designated hitter playing the Detroit Tigers. On June 13 against Tampa Bay, he became the first Japanese player in history to hit for a cycle. Hitting for a cycle means hitting a single, a double, a triple, and a home run all in the same game. It is very uncommon.

On September 12, his season came to a halt when it was announced that he needed to undergo another surgery to fix a bipartite patella.

He finished with a batting average of .286/.343/.505. He hit 18 home runs, brought in 62 runners, and stole 12 bases over the course of 106 games.

Although this was a short season for Ohtani, he still set a record and had an accomplished batting average. It was really frustrating for him to take yet another break from his sport. But injury is very common among pitchers and even the best pitchers get injured and have to take time away. It can throw curveballs in their career if they don't keep their minds straight and allow their anger to get the best of them. But Ohtani knew it was important to keep his eye on the prize and never let his frustration get in the way of preparing for his next game.

2020 Season: Another Setback

On July 24, 2020, Ohtani became history's first automatic player on second base in an official MLB game. This was at the beginning of the 10th inning as a new 2020 MLB rule. He was playing the Oakland Athletics. He got thrown out during a rundown.

On July 26, he got back on the mound playing the Oakland Athletics. It was his first time pitching since September 2018. It didn't go very well. He let in five runs and got taken off the mound without making an out. This started the season off with a loss and an infinite ERA.

After starting for the second time that season, his right arm started hurting. He had to get an MRI and it showed that he had a flexor strain located in his right elbow. The manager, Joe Maddon, revealed that he would not pitch for the remainder of the season.

His batting averages for the season were .190/.291/.366. He had 7 home runs, he brought in 24 batters, and he stole 7 bases in 43 games.

Although he made some home runs, RBIs, and stole some bases, he had a short season and didn't succeed in pitching, partially due to another injury. At this point, things were really getting frustrating for Ohtani. He had so much potential but just wasn't able to unlock it. Especially with so many injuries, it took him out of the groove and threw him off his game. But the next season would be his best yet.

2021 Season: A Season To Remember

To avoid arbitration, Ohtani signed a two-year $8.5 million contract on February 8 with the Angels.

During his first pitching playing against the Chicago White Sox on April 4, 2021, he threw almost five innings. He let in one earned run as well as two unearned runs. In those 4 ⅔ innings, he struck out seven batters. He was also the second batter in his team's lineup. He was 1 for 3. He hit a 450-foot home run solo against the first pitch he was up against.

He had to skip his start that was scheduled playing the Toronto Blue Jays because he had a blister. Instead, he had his second season start on April 20 playing the Texas Rangers. He had a 75-pitch limit. He pitched four innings with no scores, struck out seven people, and let in one hit.

For his third start on April 26 playing the Texas Rangers again, he had his first win for the season. He pitched for five innings. He let in four runs in inning one and struck out nine people. He was 2 for 3 batting and had 2 RBIs.

He was the first player in almost a century to start a game pitching with the leading number of home runs in the Majors. This had not happened since Babe

Ruth pitched the start of the game for the Yankees in 1921, with 19 home runs under his belt.

Ohtani was chosen for the 2021 Home Run Derby on June 18. This made him the first-ever pitcher and the first-ever Japanese player to be chosen. After three days, he was named the AL Player of the Week for the third time in his life after he hit six home runs and got a win as the pitcher who started the game. In another two weeks, he was named the AL Player of the Week again for the fourth time after he hit six home runs and recorded a 1.543 OPS, in addition to eight batters in six games, which helped the Angels get the record of 5-1.

On June 23, he made more history when he was a pitcher who batted for himself as a pitcher as the second batter in the lineup. At this time, designated hitter rules were in effect. That was the first time in MLB history that an American League team decided to not use a designated hitter when the National League did.

For the first time ever, he was chosen as the American League Player of the Month in June. He hit .309/.423/.889 and 13 home runs. He had a 1.312 OPS when he hit and had two wins when he pitched.

On July 3 playing the Baltimore Orioles, he was the first player in the history of the American League to get 30 home runs and 10 stolen bases during the first 81 games of the season.

On July 4, he was the first player to ever be chosen as an All-Star as both a pitcher and a position player, making history. He had already been chosen by fans to be the starting designated hitter for the 2021 All-Star Game that would take place on July 1. He was also voted by the players to be one out of five starting pitchers that made the American League roster on July 4.

On July 7, he hit his 32 home runs of the season. It was a solo home run off of the Boston Red Sox starting pitcher, Eduardo Rodriguez. This surpassed Hideki Matsui's 2004 record, making him have the largest amount of home runs in a season by a Japanese-born MLB player.

He also was the first Japanese player to win the Best Major League Baseball Player ESPY Award.

Ohtani played the Home Run Derby on July 12. During the first round of play, he hit 22 home runs, which tied him with his opponent, Juan Soto. In a tiebreaker round, they got tied again with 29 home runs. Although Soto won the second tiebreaker, Ohtani set a record of the highest number of home runs of at least 500 feet. He hit six. For his participation, he won $150,000. He donated this money to Angels support employees, like trainers, clubhouse workers, and media management. He was going to use his winning money that way no matter how much he won, he had decided.

On July 13, he once again made history during an All-Star Game as the starting pitcher as well as the designated hitter in the first spot for the American League. After he pitched a perfect inning number one, he became the first-ever player in major league history to play in the Home Run Derby and also win a game as the starting pitcher in an All-Star Game. He was also the first leadoff man to throw a fastball that was 100mph in the All-Star Game.

In his 15th start of the season pitching, on July 26, playing the Colorado Rockies, he became the first pitcher in the history of the league to throw 100 strikeouts with a major-league-leading 35 home runs before the end of July. No pitcher previously had ever gotten triple-digit strikeouts and added over nine home runs in the simultaneous season.

Also, in the same game, he became the first pitcher to pitch a top half with no scores as well as a record hit, an RBI, a stolen base, and a scored run. He achieved all of this while playing in an AL ballpark. This was the first time this happened since Luis Tiant did it while playing with the Minnesota Twins in 1970.

He finished July as the first player in the history of Major League to have at least 15 stolen bases and 37 home runs before the end of July. For the second month in a row, he won his second American League Player of the Month Award. He was the first consecutive Player of the Month Award winner in either league since 2012 when Chase Headley did so during the months of August and September, and the first in the AL since 2012 when Josh Hamilton did it.

In July, he made nine home runs, ran in 19 batters, walked 16 times, and had a .282/.396/.671 during 23 games batting. In pitching, he had a 1.35 ERA and 17 strikeouts as well as one walk in just 20 innings.

On the 19th of August, he was the first batter who is left-handed in the history of the Angels to get 40 home runs, beating Reggie Jackson's record of 39 home runs in 1982.

This was an incredible season for Ohtani and was his best one yet. He set numerous records and played in his first Home Run Derby. Even though he didn't win first place, he donated his prize money to the more underappreciated members of the Angels team, the people who make all the gameplay possible, which was a great act of respect, humbleness, and appreciation. He was finally back in the game. This is the Ohtani that everyone was waiting to see. Everyone knew it was inside of him, but injuries kept getting in the way. It just goes to show what he can do when he isn't injured. And he has so many years ahead of him as a player, especially since he renewed his contract.

The Angels are a perfect team for Ohtani because they see his talents and nurture both his hitting and pitching. They let him shine. It is impossible to know what Ohtani will do next, but whatever it is, it will be great.

SHOHEI OHTANI INTERVIEWS

When asked what he loves about baseball, he said that he would always give it his all. He hopes that by giving it his all he would be able to inspire thousands of people and make a difference in their lives if they're struggling. He wants to cheer them up with his playing. He believes that is the importance of the game of baseball.

He was asked during a press conference why he decided to change his pitching style in the middle of the game. He responded that he bases his pitching on how the hitters react, especially before they get two strikes and after they get two strikes. He usually makes this assessment during the first three innings and goes from there. He also accounts for his gut feeling on what would be the best way to approach the game.

When asked how to decide his plan of attack for a game, he said it really depends on what he's feeling during a game. He keeps track of which pitches are working and which aren't, and adjusts accordingly.

In a post-game interview, the press asked how much he thinks adding the cutter pitch has affected his game. He replied that the cutter is really helpful in keeping his pitch count lower, which is really important for pitchers in the long run to extend their career and prevent injuries.

Someone pointed out that sometimes he has a good start, but the Angels don't win. He asked Ohtani if that frustrates him. He answered that as a pitcher it is obvious that you want to win the game but that, of course, will never be the case all the time. He also said that it's important to remember that he's also part of the lineup, and if he only gets one hit in a game, he's partially to blame for the loss.

After participating in the home run derby, he was asked if it was always an event he had wanted to compete in. He said he had always wanted to participate and was ecstatic to get the invite.

When asked if he had nerves about the derby, he said he was more nervous talking to the announcers because he always saw them on TV!

He told an interviewer that he played shortstop as a young boy, but in high school, he switched to outfield.

He was asked the difference between pitching and hitting. He answered that when he's hitting he tries to analyze the pitcher's expression and body language. When pitching, he thinks about what it would be like to be the batter and what his approach would be considering the pitch count and pitches being thrown.

He was approached with a hypothetical of either not being able to pitch or not being able to hit, and if he would be as good as he is without having the insight of both. He wasn't sure because he has always been able to do both and enjoys balancing the two.

He told Mr. Pedro Martinez that growing up, he was his pitching idol.

CONCLUSION: SO WHO IS SHOHEI OHTANI?

Ohtani is incredibly humble due to his modest upbringing in an agricultural town in Japan. He is very polite in interviews. He uses an interpreter, often understanding the question in English by himself, but responding in Japanese. He is known as Japan's Babe Ruth.

As a kid, he was very adventurous. He wasn't afraid of falling on the playground. He was incredibly fast from a very young age and loved to play games like tag with his friends and classmates. It was quickly obvious that there was something special about Ohtani, and his parents wanted to nurture that.

Ohtani has two siblings, Ryuta and Yuka. Ryuta plays baseball but not professionally. He would always help Ohtani practice as kids, playing catch with him in the backyard and pitching to him so he could practice hitting. Ryuta was a bit more skittish than Ohtani. He was scared of falling or embarrassing himself, but Ohtani was more outgoing. They are still very good friends.

He grew up in a very supportive and loving household. He was taught to be caring, responsible, polite, and to work hard. He was a passionate child, which sometimes presented itself in anger. His parents worked with him to help him learn to control himself and see the good in every situation. For example, he was taught not to throw equipment if he made a mistake.

His dad was his coach in middle school for a league that was almost an hour's drive away from his house. His dad wanted to make up for being absent in Ohtani's older brother's life. He was a good coach and taught discipline as well as good form and sportsmanship.

He played shortstop primarily up until high school when he really started to focus on pitching. He also loves to play outfield. A big reason why he played with The Fighters instead of going directly to the MLB is because they were willing to let him play outfield as well as pitch. He pitches with his right hand and bats left-handed.

Ohtani has broken numerous records.

He broke the Japanese rookie home run record at 19 home runs. He threw the fastest pitch of any Japanese high schooler, clocking in at 99mph. In 2014, he threw a 101mph pitch in an All-Star Game, breaking the 2010 record of 100mph. He pitched 102.5mph, the fastest in the NPB. He tied Bobby Clark's 1979 records. He broke the Japanese rookie home run record. He hit the most home runs in one season by any Japanese-born MLB player. In the Home Run Derby, he hit six home runs of at least 500 feet, setting a new record.

Ohtani believes that sports can bring a positive change in people's lives. He understands that winding down after a long day and watching a great game of baseball can really improve someone's mood and bring them happiness and a good distraction from their problems. That is why he trains so hard and is such a good player. He knows he is doing it for himself, his team, but most importantly his fans.

MORE FROM JACKSON CARTER BIOGRAPHIES

My goal is to spark the love of reading in young adults around the world. Too often children grow up thinking they hate reading because they are forced to read material they don't care about. To counter this we offer accessible, easy to read biographies about sportspeople that will give young adults the chance to fall in love with reading.

Go to the Website Below to Join Our Community

https://mailchi.mp/7cced1339ff6/jcbcommunity

Or Find Us on Facebook at

www.facebook.com/JacksonCarterBiographies

As a Member of Our Community You Will Receive:

First Notice of Newly Published Titles

Exclusive Discounts and Offers

Influence on the Next Book Topics

Don't miss out, join today and help spread the love of reading around the world!

OTHER WORKS BY JACKSON CARTER BIOGRAPHIES

Patrick Mahomes: The Amazing Story of How Patrick Mahomes Became the MVP of the NFL

Donovan Mitchell: How Donovan Mitchell Became a Star for the Salt Lake City Jazz

Luka Doncic: The Complete Story of How Luka Doncic Became the NBA's Newest Star

The Eagle: Khabib Nurmagomedov: How Khabib Became the Top MMA Fighter and Dominated the UFC

Lamar Jackson: The Inspirational Story of How One Quarterback Redefined the Position and Became the Most Explosive Player in the NFL

Jimmy Garoppolo: The Amazing Story of How One Quarterback Climbed the Ranks to Be One of the Top Quarterbacks in the NFL

Zion Williamson: The Inspirational Story of How Zion Williamson Became the NBA's First Draft Pick

Kyler Murray: The Inspirational Story of How Kyler Murray Became the NFL's First Draft Pick

Do Your Job: The Leadership Principles that Bill Belichick and the New England Patriots Have Used to Become the Best Dynasty in the NFL

Turn Your Gaming Into a Career Through Twitch and Other Streaming Sites: How to Start, Develop and Sustain an Online Streaming Business that Makes Money

From Beginner to Pro: How to Become a Notary Public

Made in the USA
Las Vegas, NV
21 December 2023

83294447R00036